If I Really Wanted to

Simplify My Life

I would . . .

RACINE, WI

If I Really Wanted to Simplify My Life, I Would . . .
ISBN: 979-8-88898-000-2 - *Paperback*
ISBN: 979-8-88898-001-9 - *Hardcover*
ISBN: 978-1-970103-52-6 - *Ebook*
Copyright © 2022 by Honor Books
Racine, WI

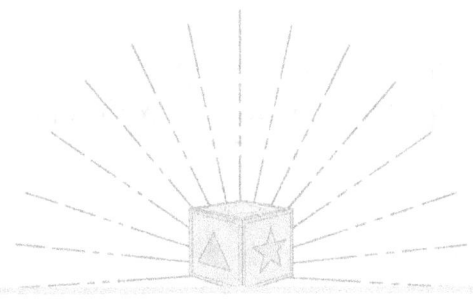

INTRODUCTION

A re you seeking a simpler life—one that allows you to pursue those things that are genuinely important? If so, then you have come to the right place.

The simple insights contained in this small book can't guarantee that your life will be less complicated—nothing can! What they can do is help you order your priorities and manage your responsibilities in a way that is more in tune with lasting values and a personal sense of well being. They may even draw you closer to the Creator and His purpose for your life.

GOD BLESS YOU IN YOUR QUEST!

IF I REALLY WANTED TO
SIMPLIFY MY LIFE, I WOULD . . .

GIVE MYSELF
PERMISSION TO
SAY "NO"

HEALTHY BOUNDARIES ALLOW US TO BE TRUE TO WHO WE ARE AND WHAT WE ARE MEANT TO DO.

We live in a society that is constantly challenging us to stretch beyond our limits and reach for the stars. Pleas for help and demands on our time and energies lie around every corner. But eventually, we each have to accept the fact that we cannot do it all. Freedom comes when we learn that such expectations are unrealistic and misguided.

Saying "no" frees you to say "yes" to those things that bring the greatest satisfaction and sense of well-being. It allows you to "de-clutter" your life and restore balance. It is the first step to leading a simpler life.

This will we do, if God permit.

HEBREWS 6:3 KJV

9

IF I REALLY WANTED TO
SIMPLIFY MY LIFE, I WOULD . . .

KEEP ONLY
ONE
CREDIT CARD

Debt and Worry are Siamese Twins.

There are few things that complicate life as completely as debt and the management thereof. So why not avoid credit cards altogether? Unfortunately, it is now impossible to rent a car, travel without carrying a large amount of cash, or carry out any one of a half dozen other functions we take for granted without at least one credit card.

So don't cut up all your credit cards—cut up all but one and use that one sparingly. Imagine your life without the stress and anxiety of worrying about unpaid bills and the hours of free time you will find when you no longer have to pour over a stack of statements. Life will be much simpler.

Always pay: for first or last you must pay your entire debt.

Ralph W. Emerson

CLEAN OUT
MY CLOSETS

GIVE WHAT YOU CANNOT USE TO GAIN WHAT YOU CANNOT BUY!

I tems that have been stored in your closets for more than a year are merely taking up space and making it more difficult to find the things you need. So what can you do with all those "don't quite fit," "not exactly new," "way too good to throw away" items?

There are many wonderful non-profit agencies that can provide a way to put those annoying leftovers to good use across the nation and around the world. Chances are there is one such enterprise near you. Cleaning out your closets can lighten your load and allow you the pleasure of knowing you are helping to meet the needs of others—a wonderfully liberating experience.

We make a living by what we get, but we make a life by what we give.

WINSTON CHURCHILL

ALWAYS TELL THE TRUTH, THE WHOLE TRUTH, AND NOTHING BUT THE TRUTH

IT'S NEVER WRONG TO BE SIMPLE TRUTHFUL.

L ies not only create breaches of trust, they cause an inner decay as well. Truth, in contrast, builds a foundation for all other aspects of character. It establishes your personal integrity and becomes the cornerstone for your lasting relationships.

It's never wrong to be simply truthful.

The educator Horace Mann once gave this good advice: "Keep one thing forever in view—the truth; and if you do this, although it may seem to lead you away from the opinions of men, it will assuredly conduct you to the throne of God." Always speak the truth—not just part of it, but all of it. And remember to be kind and compassionate as you do so.

Truth is tough. It will not break like a bubble at the touch, nay, you may kick it about all day like a football and it will be round and full at evening.

OLIVER WENDELL HOLMES JR.

KEEP A ROLLING GROCERY LIST

EVERYTHING IS EASIER WITH A PLAN.

Have you ever had three or four essential items come to mind while you were putting away the groceries you just purchased? Have you ever brought home duplicate items because you couldn't remember what you bought on your last shopping trip? Those little cognitive glitches can be costly, time consuming, and frustrating.

Try keeping a notepad and a pen in the kitchen dedicated solely to grocery items and give all members of the household access to it. Your list then serves as a handy tour guide for your next shopping extravaganza. Imagine coming home with no duplicate purchases and no forgotten items—simply delightful!

The plans of the diligent lead to profit as surely as haste leads to poverty.

PROVERBS 21:5

TAKE TIME OFF TO RENEW MY ENERGY AND CREATIVITY

A SIMPLE LIFE IS A BALANCED LIFE.

Work and leisure are two sides of the same coin—fulfillment and satisfaction in life. We can get thrown off balance if we neglect either one. Work makes us feel needed and productive, and it is essential to health and happiness. But overwork is counterproductive and dehumanizing. Both our bodies and minds need time and rest.

Take some time away the next time you need a fresh perspective and a renewed appreciation for your work and those you work with. It's a winning situation for everyone. You will come back a "kinder and gentler" version of yourself, more capable, more creative, and more gracious to others.

Even the soil becomes depleted if it tries to produce without a season of rest.

T. D. JAKES

Get Regular Physical and Dental Check-Ups

SMALL PROBLEMS ARE NEARLY ALWAYS EASIER TO RESOLVE THAN LARGE ONES.

Medical and dental emergencies can be costly, time-consuming, and painful. Weigh the expense of such an incident against the time and money it takes to visit your doctor and dentist for regular check-ups. You will find that prevention is a bargain.

The most important thing, however, is to consider what your life would be like if you should be stricken with a life-threatening illness or condition. Early detection can mean the difference between life and death. Do all you can while you can to keep your life unencumbered by the stress and hardship of ill health.

Life is not merely being alive but being well.

MARTIAL

FILL UP THE TANK WHEN IT'S HALF FULL

NOBODY CAN DRIVE ON FUMES.

A full tank gives peace of mind and prevents frustration, especially when you are pressed for time. The same is true in most areas of life—a full measure provides a greater sense of wellbeing than a half measure. Tell the whole story, eat an entire well-balanced meal at one sitting without interruptions, enjoy the total experience, remember all that is pertinent and helpful. When dealing with tasks, doing the entire job is more rewarding than leaving it half undone.

Don't subject yourself to unnecessary complications. You can minimize risk and simplify your life by using just a dash of common sense and foresight.

Prevention is the daughter of intelligence.

SIR WALTER RALEIGH

BUY CHRISTMAS GIFTS ALL YEAR LONG

THE BEST CHRISTMAS GIFT WE CAN GIVE OURSELVES IS TIME.

By the time Christmas Day rolls around each year, many of us find that we are too exhausted and too broke to enjoy the celebration. That's because we have spent the two or three weeks before Christmas in a flurry of baking, cleaning, decorating, signing cards, and buying and wrapping gifts.

Try purchasing two or three gifts a month throughout the year. Wrap and label them so that you can remember what they are and who they are for. Christmas cards can be signed and addressed well in advance also. This approach makes life a little simpler and saves you money. Cards and gifts are much less expensive in January than in December.

Commit to the Lord whatever you do, and your plans will succeed.

PROVERBS 16:3

CHOOSE HOUSEPLANTS THAT DON'T REQUIRE MUCH CARE

STREAMLINING CARE DOES NOT MEAN SACRIFICING BEAUTY.

Houseplants are a great way to keep the air fresh, the room cheery in any season, and our lives connected to the out-of-doors and God's greater creation. But they also demand attention to survive.

Ivies, such as pothos and philodendron, and succulents, such as aloe and cactus, are plants that can go for long periods without watering or care. In the darker areas of your home, consider the use of silk plants—all they require is an occasional trip to the shower to remove the dust. It is possible to have all the benefits of indoor plants without letting them complicate your life.

A thing of beauty is a joy forever; its loveliness increases; it will never pass into nothingness.

JOHN KEATS

IF I REALLY WANTED TO
SIMPLIFY MY LIFE, I WOULD . . .

PUT THINGS BACK WHERE I GOT THEM

ORGANIZATION CREATES HARMONY AND LESSENS STRESS.

W ho can fully calculate the time wasted looking for misplaced keys, tickets, or eyeglasses; records needed for tax preparation, appliance warranties, or the other sock, shoe, or earring? Returning something to its place turns out to be an amazing investment when you think of it that way.

Save yourself from the stress and frustration of searching for what you need. Designate a place for each and every item and send it home each time you use it. You will be amazed how much simpler it will be to make a repair when you know where to find a screwdriver or a hammer.

No pain, no gain.

UNKNOWN

IF I REALLY WANTED TO
SIMPLIFY MY LIFE, I WOULD . . .

KEEP ONLY
ONE
DAY-PLANNER
OR CALENDAR

WRITE IT DOWN ... ONCE.

Find a style and format that works and use that method to record all your important dates, appointments, and key facts. If you have one planner for work and another for social appointments, you are likely to overlook conflicts and miss important dates.

It's also wise to have only one family calendar or planner for recording events and obligations that involve one or more family members. You can avoid disappointments by realizing that no one can be in two places at the same time. So do yourself a favor. Write it down in one place where the whole family can see what's up. Life is complicated enough, why cultivate confusion!

Time is the coin of your life. It is the only coin you have and only you can determine how it is spent.

CARL SANDBURG

WATCH AND LEARN FROM THOSE WHO ARE EXPERTS

IF YOU WANT TO LEARN HOW TO DO SOMETHING RIGHT, START BY WATCHING SOMEONE WHO DOES IT RIGHT.

The reason life-designer Martha Stewart is so popular could be that we are fascinated by watching other people do things well. Haven't you ever been mesmerized watching Olympic athletes, world-class musicians and artists, renowned chefs, the local expert auto mechanic, or some other true professional use his or her talents?

A highly mastered skill is a picture of both quality and efficiency—mistakes are generally few, and rarely is any motion or effort wasted. Rather than bemoan a lack of expertise, choose to watch experts more closely, pick up pointers, and then practice. "Watch" and "learn" are action words for any eager learner.

Do you see a man skilled in his work? He will serve before kings.

PROVERBS 22:29

GET PLENTY OF SLEEP

LEARN TO VIEW SLEEP AS A GIFT FROM YOUR CREATOR.

During sleep the brain stays busy sorting and storing information, replenishing chemicals, and resolving problems or inequities. Scientists are not exactly sure how all this happens, but they are amazed by the amount and variety of activity that occurs while the body is at rest.

To get the most out of sleep hours, scientists recommend that you keep regular sleeping hours, get sufficient and regular exercise, quit smoking, limit caffeine, and refrain from overeating before going to bed. Sufficient rest will keep you at your best and make all your efforts more productive and more enjoyable.

Sleep is sweet to the laboring man.

JOHN BUNYAN

IDENTIFY MY MOST PRODUCTIVE TIME OF DAY AND MAXIMIZE IT

FIND OUT WHAT MAKES YOU TICK AND LIVE YOUR LIFE ACCORDINGLY.

Metabolisms vary, energy levels ebb and flow, and body rhythms fluctuate. The key to maximizing efficiency and productivity is to work with your own natural internal body rhythms. Schedule the most challenging tasks when energy is at a peak level. Do creative work during the time of day when creativity seems abundant. Don't let anything interfere with these important hours—making the most of them can be a key to success.

When energy and creativity begin to wane, take a break or switch to more routine chores. And when you feel you need a nap, take one.

Make it thy business to know thyself.

MIGUEL DE CERVANTES

ESTABLISH
A SHOES-OFF-IN-
THE-HOUSE
POLICY

THE BEST PLACE FOR THE VACUUM IS IN ITS CLOSET.

An old floor wax commercial presented this timeless message: "Kids! When it comes to floors, how they hurt you so. Kids! They leave lots of heel marks, as you well know." Whether it's a hard-surface floor or a carpet, it needs to be cleaned. But cleaning is easier and less frequent if dirt and grime are left outside rather than tracked inside.

Not only does a shoes-off-in-the-house rule save time and effort, but also cleaning products and frustration. If shoes must be worn, make sure they are wiped thoroughly on a mat outside the house. If children are barefoot, make sure their feet are clean before they come inside. The same goes for the dog's paws!

Housework can't kill you, but why take a chance.

PHYLLIS DILLER

IF I REALLY WANTED TO
SIMPLIFY MY LIFE, I WOULD . . .

KEEP A
REGULAR
ROUTINE

THE UNIVERSE WAS CREATED TO RUN ON A PREDICTABLE, ORDERLY SCHEDULE. WE WERE, TOO!

Expert gardeners know that tomato plants need to be staked and climbing vines need a trellis to achieve optimal growth. Without adequate physical support, some plants are quick to collapse and wither. We human beings are like plants in this way. We also need structure and support to be at our personal best.

Some of that structure and support can be obtained by developing and following a regular pattern of health habits, such as daily exercise, sufficient sleep, and good nutrition breaks several times a day. Organizing your time and activities promotes a sense of well being.

There is a time for everything, and a season for every activity under heaven.

ECCLESIASTES 3:1

BUY CARRY-OUT AND USE DELIS WHEN I'M ENTERTAINING

CREATIVITY AND SIMPLICITY ARE THE KEYS TO HEARTWARMING HOSPITALITY.

Have you ever worked so hard to prepare for company that you found yourself exhausted and cranky by the time the guests arrived? When hospitality becomes a burden, those you intended to bless lose their sense of feeling at home. So how do you get ready without all the stress?

For starters, forget the notion that the house must be perfect. Pick up a bouquet of fresh flowers and light some candles to create a homey atmosphere. Instead of cooking for hours, make use of convenient prepared foods available at delis and most supermarkets. Simple, gracious meals and a comfortable environment are all you need to make your guests feel welcome and cared for.

Quality is never an accident. It represents the choice of many alternatives.

WILLA A. FOSTER

43

Keep a Master Gift-Giving List in my Wallet

GIFT SHOPPING CAN BE FUN AGAIN!

Have you ever noticed how much easier it is to find a gift when you're not looking for one? Keep your gift-giving list with you at all times and you will have all you need to shop for birthday, holiday, and anniversary gifts as you go. The best way to keep things straight is to create a grid and tuck it into your wallet.

As items are purchased, note the name of the person the gift is for, the occasion when the gift will be given, the price, and where you purchased it. Tape the receipt to the gift and store it in a single designated drawer, cupboard, or closet shelf so it can be found quickly when needed. As gifts are given, cross them off the list.

Direction literally creates time.

ZIG ZIGLAR

45

IF I REALLY WANTED TO
SIMPLIFY MY LIFE, I WOULD . . .

DELEGATE,
DELEGATE,
DELEGATE

MANY HANDS TRULY DO MAKE LIGHT WORK.

N o person can do all or be all. That's why eventually we each reach the conclusion that we must share responsibility with others. And after all, sharing work often makes it more fun. Whenever possible, include others in your planning rather than waiting until the last moment.

Of course, there will be tasks that only you can do, but developing a team spirit concerning those tasks that can be shared will alleviate frustration, resentment, and physical exhaustion. To delegate successfully, be willing to trust others to complete a job. Allow for errors—don't expect perfection, and be quick to give rewards and praise.

It is amazing what you can accomplish if you don't care who gets the credit.

HARRY S. TRUMAN

IF I REALLY WANTED TO
SIMPLIFY MY LIFE, I WOULD . . .

BUY ALL THE BIRTHDAY AND ANNIVERSARY CARDS FOR A GIVEN MONTH AT ONE TIME

Buying a single greeting card is sometimes as time-consuming as buying a pair of shoes! Consider an alternative method: On the first shopping day of the month, review the family date book and make a card-shopping list. Choose a card store with a large selection. Then evaluate each card with several different people in mind.

You will do even better if you can buy for a three-month period at one time. When you get them home, sit down and sign each card. Address the envelopes, but don't seal them. You may want to add something at the last minute.

Those who plan what is good find love and
faithfulness.

PROVERBS 14:22

IF I REALLY WANTED TO
SIMPLIFY MY LIFE, I WOULD . . .

STOP TRYING TO KEEP UP WITH THE JONESES

THE RACE TO ACQUIRE MORE IS A NEVER-ENDING RACE.

So often we are tempted to define our lives by what we own and how much we possess in comparison with other people. The standard may not be the Joneses—it may be the ideal of the "good life" or the examples of affluence we see on television and in the movies. The snare to "have it all" can result in entrapment to debt and the emotional bondage of low self-esteem. Balance and moderation slide away when greed sets in.

Choose instead to establish your self-worth on the basis of virtue and character. It is also important to make a distinction between wants and needs, and to be grateful for what is rather than grieving for what isn't.

Things which matter most should never be at the mercy of things which matter least.

JOHANN WOLFGANG VON GOETHE

KEEP AN EXTRA CAR KEY IN MY WALLET OR UNDER THE BUMPER OF MY CAR

SAFE ENTRANCE IS ALWAYS SIMPLER THAN EMERGENCY RESCUE.

Being locked out of your car is never convenient or desirable, especially if the motor is running or there is a child or handicapped person inside. Calling a locksmith or breaking a window is expensive and time consuming. Keeping an extra car key taped to a card in your wallet or placing an extra key in a magnetic box under the bumper of your car can ensure access and provide peace of mind.

Having an extra set of car keys in the house can also be a life saver when your primary set does a disappearing act and you are left with no keys and no time. A similar policy for house keys can also be a blessing.

True wisdom consists not only in seeing what is before your eyes, but in foreseeing what is to come.

TERRENCE

LEARN TO USE A CROCK POT

TWO TASKS IN ONE TIME FRAME CAN MEAN MORE TIME TO ENJOY YOUR LIFE.

Cooking with a crock pot allows for meal preparation to occur simultaneously with work, chores, or family fun. Many things in life can be done in similar two-for-one fashion. Use drive time for listening to inspirational or educational tapes. Use chores as an opportunity to interact with other family members. Let children practice math skills as part of a trip to the grocery store. Memorize scriptures while working out at the gym.

Look for ways to do two good things at once, without sacrificing quality in either task. You can pack more meaning into a day with less effort.

Dost thou love life? Then do not squander time, for that's the stuff life is made of.

BENJAMIN FRANKLIN

AVOID
BORROWING
FROM
OTHERS

No Borrowing? No Remembering to Pay Back!

Borrowing and lending are an intricate part of the human equation. Your emphasis, however, should always be on lending. Those who borrow excessively, fail to return what they borrow in a timely manner, or return borrowed items in disrepair complicate their own lives and the lives of others.

Borrowing is necessary at times, but careless borrowing can damage relationships, create guilt, and cause a backlash of anger and resentment. So think twice before you borrow anything from anyone. And if you do find yourself on the borrowing end, save yourself a lot of grief by being a conscientious borrower.

For the Lord your God will bless you as he has promised, and you will lend to many nations but will borrow from none.

Deuteronomy 15:6

Keep a Separate Set of Toiletries and Personal Items in my Suitcase

BEING HALF-PACKED AT ALL TIMES MEANS YOU CAN BE READY IN HALF THE TIME.

If you spend much time traveling for work or pleasure, you can appreciate how much time and effort is wasted packing and unpacking for a trip. You can simplify the process by keeping a complete set of trial or travel-sized toiletries packed in their own case and placed permanently in your suitcase. Don't put your suitcase away until all used-up items in the kit have been replaced.

You might also consider keeping an extra set of small travel appliances, such as a hair dryer, as well as a duplicate round of vitamins and medications in your suitcase. Finally, for quick reference keep a list of basic clothing items that generally are needed for each trip.

Whatever you're ready for is ready for you.

MARK VICTOR HANSEN

IF I REALLY WANTED TO
SIMPLIFY MY LIFE, I WOULD . . .

SIGN UP FOR AN AUTOMATIC SAVINGS PLAN

Quit planning to save. Start saving—and Plan!

The best and simplest way to save money is to see that it never reaches your checking account. If you find it difficult to put money aside, ask your employer or bank to deduct a portion of your paycheck and place it into a retirement or savings account. The results can be astounding.

If you set aside only fifty dollars a month, you will have $3,000 in just five years—perhaps more. Those who already have a sufficient amount in savings or a retirement fund might consider starting a savings account for charitable giving. Worthy ministries and charities can always use a helping hand.

More people should learn to tell their dollars where to go instead of asking them where they went.

Roger Babson

READ INSTRUCTIONS AND FOLLOW THEM

THOSE WHO CHOOSE TO LIVE WISELY LIVE WELL.

You can avoid a tremendous amount of frustration and conflict by taking time to read through the instructions before beginning any project. Toys go together more quickly. Recipes usually taste better. Projects are accomplished with greater efficiency and quality. Though you may not want to admit it, working without reading the instructions is like trying to find your way to Kansas without a road map.

Many efforts fail or fall short of their potential solely for lack of information. Don't let that happen to you. Get the best information available, and then apply it. You'll be glad you did.

There are three things you should do
when you make a mistake:

1. Admit it

2. Learn from it

3. Read the instructions

ANONYMOUS

PLAN AND SAVE FOR FAMILY VACATIONS IN ADVANCE

ANTICIPATING IS HALF THE FUN!

Planning a family vacation together can be great fun and a hedge against disappointment and unrealistic expectations. Hold a family meeting about six months in advance of the trip. Ask someone to take notes and then let everyone offer ideas and discuss them freely. Assign research tasks and plan another meeting in one month.

It's also a good idea to ask each family member to find ways of saving money for the trip. Keep vacation funds separate from regular savings or checking accounts. Help children begin their own vacation funds to pay for souvenirs and special treats. When everyone feels some ownership in the plans, you will have a lot more fun and a lot less stress.

Commit to the Lord whatever you do, and your plans will succeed.

PROVERBS 16:3

REFUSE TO
SPEND WHAT
I DON'T HAVE

TO KEEP BOOKKEEPING SIMPLE—DECIDE ON A PLAN AND STICK WITH IT!

Overextending your credit limits or making purchases you can't afford are practices with big price tags attached. Once you fall behind and interest begins to accrue, you have entered a crisis-driven, high-anxiety disaster zone. What a headache!

Establishing a budget may seem like hard work but the reality is that it frees you, simplifies financial management, and gives you priceless peace of mind. Once you've calculated your budget, set aside the money needed to pay regular bills—including a contribution for savings—and then pay cash for purchases with your remaining funds. Make sure all bills related to needs are paid before shopping for wants.

It's hard to pay for bread that has already been eaten.

DANISH PROVERB

SHOP WHEN THE STORES ARE LESS CROWDED

SHOP WHEN OTHERS DON'T.

S topping to shop on the drive home from work may seem like a time-saving strategy, especially if the store is on the way. However, if you work 8:00 to 5:00, you will quickly find that a great many other people had the same idea. Traffic and long lines aren't the only problems you will encounter. Your resistance to impulse buying is also lower because your energy level is at a low ebb.

This is especially true in a food store. Stores are far less crowded and service is generally better early in the morning when stores first open. Shopping at off times can save you time, frustration, and in many cases, money.

Either you run your day, or your day runs you!

JIM ROHN

Give Myself a Break

ASKING FOR HELP IS NOT A SIGN
OF WEAKNESS; IT IS A SIGN OF
SANITY.

Many people today find themselves precariously stretched between home, career, and miscellaneous other obligations. This delicate balance may include caring for elderly parents, small children, or someone who is disabled. Whatever the hand you have been dealt, you will play it better if you learn to care for your own needs.

Help is easier to find if you plan ahead. Find a children's or seniors' program in your area that can provide you with a few hours of down time and locate someone to help with the laundry and cleaning at least once a week. If money is an issue, it may be possible to exchange these services with a friend or neighbor.

Run if you like but try to keep your breath;
work like a man but don't be worked to death.

OLIVER WENDELL HOLMES

KEEP MY
PROMISES

BE CAREFUL WHAT YOU PROMISE TO DELIVER, AND YOU WILL BE ABLE TO DELIVER WHAT YOU PROMISE.

People who keep their promises don't have to look over their shoulders with regret and guilt. They have earned the trust and respect of others. Those who do not keep their promises live with broken relationships, unmet expectations, and all the problems that accompany a lack of integrity.

Don't complicate your life by making promises you can't keep or breaking the promises you do make. Think twice before saying, "I'll be there," or "I'll take care of that." If you are worried about hurting someone's feelings by saying "no," think how much worse that person will feel if you make a promise and then can't carry through.

Do not break your oath.

MATTHEW 5:33

73

TOUCH MAIL
ONLY ONCE
AFTER BRINGING
IT IN FROM
THE MAILBOX

DEAL DIRECTLY WITH LIFE AS IT COMES YOUR WAY.

C lose your eyes and you can almost hear your mother say, "Stop fiddlin' with that." And yet, if you are like most people, you continue to fiddle with things, revisiting them too many times before actually dealing with them. This not only includes the mail—which a person may touch, move, or review a number of times before tossing the junk, answering the letter, and paying the bills—but also ideas, painful memories, and dreams.

Declutter the desk of your mind! Let go . . . resolve . . . answer . . . pay . . . decide. Free yourself to enjoy the present moment as fully as possible.

You can't have a better tomorrow if you're thinking about yesterday all the time.

CHARLES F. KETTERING

COOK TWICE AS MUCH FOR DINNER AND FREEZE HALF

A LITTLE EXTRA ALONG THE WAY CAN SAVE YOU A LOT DOWN THE ROAD!

Preparing a healthy meal for your family seems like the least you can do for the people you love. The problem is that today's lifestyles don't often lend themselves to this ideal, especially for working parents. Guilt and frustration seem to be constantly on the menu.

You can win this battle by remembering this one small trick. When you do cook, double the recipe and freeze half for a future meal. This simple strategy will not cost you a penny more and is guaranteed to keep you basking in the sweet satisfaction of knowing you have done right by the people you care about the most.

Mothers, food, love, and career, the four major guilt groups.

CATHY GUISEWITE

TRAVEL LIGHT

Let Go of the Extraneous!

There are so many advantages to traveling light—less to carry, fewer things to keep track of, fewer items to wash, iron, clean, or repair; fewer things to buy, which means less pressure to earn and spend; in general, a greater sense of freedom.

So what are the disadvantages? You're afraid you might end up needing that pink skirt or lime green dress shirt? Traveling light may decrease your personal choices somewhat, but it will also free you from the stress of unnecessary decisions, increasing your focus on the important things and providing greater flexibility. Try it. You may well wonder how you ever did it any other way.

Simplicity is making the journey of life with just enough baggage.

Charles Warner

TURN OFF THE TELEVISION AND FEED THE SOUL

YOU ARE WHAT YOU EAT.

There are many types of "soul food"— reading a book, watching the sun set, spending time with a friend, or just listening intently to the rhythm of life. These and many other nutritious activities are known to feed our desire for truth and other noble, beautiful, and virtuous ideals. Sadly, we too often settle for "junk soul food" like watching television.

A constant diet of television's fare may be easy but it certainly is not simple. Too much television can muddle and confuse your sense of morality, ethics, and virtue. It can stunt your ability to think and create and inhibit your spiritual growth. Look for activities that build up and cause an active mental or creative response.

He who gets wisdom loves his own soul; he who cherishes understanding prospers.

PROVERBS 19:8

ADDRESS SMALL PROBLEMS BEFORE THEY BECOME DISASTERS

IF LEFT TO THEMSELVES, MOLEHILLS CAN GROW INTO MOUNTAINS.

Minor irritations rarely go away on their own. Instead they have a way of transforming themselves into great, big, complicated messes. If you have a loose button on your shirt, ignore it and sure enough, it will fall off in the middle of a business meeting. If your toilet won't stop running, no need to get excited—until next month's water bill arrives. Your car is making a strange sound? Ignore it, and it's likely to leave you stranded in the middle of a four-lane highway.

Putting off the remedy to minor irritants only gives them an opportunity to become complicated problems. Simplify your future by dealing directly with the present.

The future is purchased by the present.

SAMUEL JOHNSON

IF I REALLY WANTED TO SIMPLIFY MY LIFE, I WOULD . . .

LIVE IN THE PRESENT

TAKE YOUR LIFE OFF HOLD AND LIVE EACH DAY TO THE FULLEST.

I t is wise to prepare for what the future holds and foolish to indulge in worry, regrets, and anger over the past. Such a futile and disagreeable path can rob you of present happiness.

Choose instead to live each day to the fullest, confident that God holds you securely and safely in His hands. Forgive yourself and forgive others. Don't drag the hurts and disappointments of yesterday into your today. And don't let the sun go down on today without wiping the slate clean for a better tomorrow. You have no power to change the past—only the future.

Why worry? If you've done the very best you can, worrying won't make it any better.

WALT DISNEY

LEARN FROM THE PAST

ENHANCE YOUR FUTURE BY LEARNING FROM YOUR PAST.

Some people long to return to the "good ol' days." But living in the past can enslave you to a long list of regrets and "what ifs." If the past is good for anything, it is to help you understand the present and give you the power to shape the future.

So when your mind wanders to the past, don't let it become ensnared, but use those memories to carve out an advantage. By studying your failures, you can greatly increase your chances for success in a future endeavor. By studying the causes of your unsuccessful relationships, you can become a better friend, spouse, etc. By reviewing your mistakes, you can learn to make better choices.

I will remember the deeds of the Lord; yes, I will remember your miracles of long ago.

PSALM 77:11

IF I REALLY WANTED TO
SIMPLIFY MY LIFE, I WOULD . . .

TAKE THE
SCENIC
ROUTE
HOME

YOU CAN TURN THE WHEEL TOWARD A MORE SERENE EXPERIENCE.

Whenever possible, take the back road home, especially if it's less congested and has a more scenic view. The route may take a few minutes longer, but you are almost certain to find that the absence of exhaust fumes and road rage make it well worth the investment.

Back roads tend to have fewer billboards and store signs. They remind us of simpler times and places. Find a less-traveled road home from work in the afternoon and watch the complex problems of the day melt away. Add some soothing music or the company of a friend, and you will arrive home a kinder and gentler human being.

Don't worry. Don't hurry, and don't forget to take time to smell the flowers.

CHARLES "TREMENDOUS" JONES

KEEP RECEIPTS AND TAX INFORMATION IN ONE PLACE

Plan now or pay later!

D on't wait until you are facing an IRS audit or up against a tax deadline to try to find and organize receipts. That's a mistake that will lead you down a long, frustrating, and costly road. Do yourself a favor and don't go there!

Keep your financial papers organized and in a place where you can access them quickly. Something as simple as an accordion file can be a great help in sorting and storing tax deductible receipts and other pertinent information. Remember to do this even if someone else is preparing your return. No matter who fills out the forms, you will be asked to provide the information. A little bit of forethought can save you a big headache.

But in this world nothing is certain but death and taxes.

Benjamin Franklin

AVOID SUBSCRIBING TO MAGAZINES AND NEWSPAPERS I DON'T HAVE TIME TO READ

FEW PEOPLE TRULY HAVE TIME TO "READ ALL ABOUT IT!"

Current or recent issues of magazines and newspapers are hard to throw away. Somehow we feel we will miss a vital nugget of information if we don't at least skim the pages. The result can be a mountain of paper-shuffled, reshuffled, and occasionally dusted.

You can alleviate the guilt and simplify the process by subscribing only to those periodicals that you really want to read and actually have time to read. The best approach is to read magazines and newspapers as soon as they arrive. As soon as the new one arrives, pitch the old one into a recycling bin. If you find something you want to keep, make a copy, label and date it, and file it.

I took a speed-reading course and read War and Peace in twenty minutes. It involves Russia.

WOODY ALLEN

IF I REALLY WANTED TO
SIMPLIFY MY LIFE, I WOULD . . .

JOIN A CAR POOL

SIMPLIFY YOUR LIFE BY SHARING IT.

One of the best ways to simplify your life is to share resources with others. Car pools, baby-sitting co-ops, and food cooperatives are three of the best. Work with family members and friends to discover more ways you might combine your efforts. Communities are built and enriched, when their members share meals, work on community-benefit projects together, and pitch in and help one another in both good times and bad.

When you invest your energies in league with others, you will find that those efforts are multiplied many fold and you have an added bonus—the knowledge that you have helped others to simplify their lives as well.

Let each of you look out not only for his own interests, but also for the interests of others.

PHILIPPIANS 2:4 NKJV

IF I REALLY WANTED TO
SIMPLIFY MY LIFE, I WOULD . . .

REFUSE TO GET INVOLVED IN OFFICE POLITICS

POLITICS ARE NINETY PERCENT TALK, AND NINETY PERCENT OF THE TALK IS UNPRODUCTIVE.

At the root of office politics is a quest for more power and a desire to use personal power for your own advantage. It is fueled by a "me first" attitude. The best way to avoid being a victim of the manipulative and competitive efforts of others is to refuse to play the game. Avoid gossip, and speak well of co-workers. Listen closely to instructions and goals that relate to the good of all, rather than focusing on personal agendas. And always refuse to engage in activities that may bring personal harm to the status or reputation of another.

When you rise above the muck and mire, you'll find a simpler strata in which to work.

Hear no ill of a friend, nor speak any of an enemy.

BENJAMIN FRANKLIN

If I really wanted to
Simplify my life, i would . . .

Keep a
Well-Stocked
Sewing Kit and
Toolbox

BEING READY KEEPS LIFE STEADY.

Have you ever wasted an hour looking for a needle, the measuring tape, or the scissors? A well-stocked sewing kit can make a number of small, practical tasks possible without fruitless searches and long delays. A well-stocked tool box is worth its weight in gold when you need to hang a picture or replace the faucet in the kitchen sink. A fully equipped office can make work flow faster and more efficiently, and a well-stocked cupboard can save your sanity when unexpected guests drop by.

Having what you need on hand allows for immediate flexibility and productivity in many dimensions of life.

Before everything else, getting ready is the secret of success.

HENRY FORD

LET BYGONES BE BYGONES

FORGIVING WRONGS IS THE RIGHT THING TO DO.

The secret to avoiding a lifetime of frustration and an old age marked by bitterness is simple: don't hold onto hurts and offenses. No one sets out to hold a grudge, but it's easy to get caught up in a confrontation and trigger a cycle of emotional hurt. From there, it takes determination to keep your soul swept clean, but the effort is well worth it if you want to lead a simple, uncomplicated life.

Holding a grudge can cause you to doubt the sincerity of others, avoid getting close to people, overreact to perceived slights, and become irritable, petty, and paranoid. Life is too short, no matter what its span, to hold a grudge.

You can't get ahead while you're getting even.

RICHARD K. ARMEY

LISTEN MORE AND TALK LESS

Mum's a GOOD word.

What you don't say can't complicate your life. That may be the very reason God gave us two ears and only one mouth! Prove this to yourself by making a conscious effort to listen twice as much as you speak. You may well find that it is more difficult than you imagined.

The best tactic is to find a middle ground somewhere between syllables and silence. Practice thinking before you speak rather than after and remember that when you avoid speaking carelessly, you also avoid hurt feelings, embarrassing gaffes, and misunderstandings. This is especially true if you are learning to listen intently at the same time.

A man of knowledge uses words with restraint.

PROVERBS 17:27

BUY CLOTHES
I CAN MIX
AND MATCH

THE TWO BEST FASHION ACCESSORIES ARE ALWAYS THESE: A BRIGHT SMILE AND INNER BEAUTY.

Do you sometimes feel as if you have a closet full of clothes, but nothing to wear? Consultants routinely advise that the best idea is to build your wardrobe around classic clothing that can be mixed and matched. Invest in a blazer, skirt, and pants—or for men, a suit, sports coat, and slacks. Then coordinate the basics with interchangeable print blouses or shirts. Finally, add coordinating accessories and two pairs of shoes, one for casual wear and the other for more formal occasions.

Each season, additional color-coordinated items can be added until the mix and match possibilities are virtually endless. Why clutter your closet and your life with faddish, standalone outfits?

In character, in manner, in style, in all things, the supreme excellence is simplicity.

HENRY WADSWORTH LONGFELLOW

IF I REALLY WANTED TO
SIMPLIFY MY LIFE, I WOULD . . .

PICK UP
AFTER
MYSELF

CLEAN A LITTLE NOW OR A LOT LATER. IT'S UP TO YOU.

Some people actually enjoy housecleaning, but for most of us it's an arduous and time-consuming chore. It will seem a lot less intimidating, however, if you tackle it by the inch rather than by the mile.

You can do that with a discipline as simple as picking up after yourself. Rinse off dishes and place them in the dishwasher as soon as you are finished with them. Undress in the closet where you can hang up your clothes as you take them off. Place dirty clothing directly into the hamper. Put things back where you found them and don't start projects you don't have the energy to clean up.

What may he done at any time will he done at no time.

THOMAS FULLER, M.D.

DECORATE WITH EASY CARE IN MIND

CHOOSE TO MAKE A HOME, RATHER THAN AN IMPRESSION.

Decorating your home with maintenance in mind need not mean sacrificing color, quality, texture, comfort, or beauty. Easy care simply means choosing fabrics and surfaces that can be easily cleaned and that stand up to wear. It means choosing items for use over appearance.

If the care is easy, housekeeping takes less time, which leaves more time for family fun and doing the things you really enjoy. And easy care choices result in less concern over spills and traffic through the house. When you design and decorate for easy-care living, you are generally making choices with the comfort, ease, and feelings of others in mind.

A sparkling house is a fine thing if the children aren't robbed of their luster in keeping it that way.

MARCELENE COX

IF I REALLY WANTED TO SIMPLIFY MY LIFE, I WOULD . . .

KEEP A RUNNING "JOB JAR"

MANAGE YOUR WORK OR YOUR WORK WILL MANAGE YOU!

I f you're like most people, you come in each night, look around and say, "Boy, I sure need to fix that," or "Gosh, this needs painting." The trouble is those things never really get done until they fall down or create a crisis.

Don't let such tasks overwhelm you— keep a "job jar." When one of those "fix me up" needs comes to mind, write it down on a piece of paper and estimate the time needed to complete the task. One morning a month, pull out a job that you can complete in the available time frame. You'll be amazed at how much can be accomplished by making maximum use of a few hours of down time.

The plans of the diligent lead surely to plenty.

PROVERBS 21:5 NKJV

KEEP ADDRESSES AND TELEPHONE NUMBERS IN ONE PLACE

INFORMATION YOU CAN'T FIND IS INFORMATION YOU CAN'T USE.

Anyone who has experience with record keeping and information processing knows that keeping track of data can be a challenge. A misplaced file can cost you an hour's worth of searching with no guarantee of success. A phone number written on a scrap of paper and misplaced on a cluttered desk can lead you to the brink of madness.

The basic rule of thumb is this: organize the information or files in such a way that there is only one place an item should be filed. Make sure the telephone and address lists in your personal phone directory are current, and then put the list in one likely place. Leave it there permanently and store or discard old address books.

Be regular and orderly in your life so that you may be violent and original in your work.

GUSTAVE FLAUBERT

IF I REALLY WANTED TO SIMPLIFY MY LIFE, I WOULD . . .

MAKE LISTS

Written Lists Can Give You Back Your Confidence.

If you pride yourself on being able to remember every detail, remember these words: "Good Luck." That's what you will need, especially as you age. Making lists—of things to buy, events to remember, projects and chores to do—may not be as compelling for the ego, but it is guaranteed to declutter your mind and create an environment where you are more efficient and less likely to make errors.

Written lists make prioritizing easier and planning simple. They can help you make wiser decisions, think through a project more exactly, communicate more clearly, and organize more effectively. Plus, marking things off a list can create an internal sense of reward.

Our memories are card indexes consulted, and then put hack in disorder by authorities we do not control.

Cyril Connolly

HELP WHEN I CAN, BUT TRY NOT TO OWN OTHER PEOPLE'S PROBLEMS

WE ALL HAVE OUR LIVES TO LIVE!

When someone needs help, advice, or simply an ear to bend, listen objectively and empathetically. Allow others to fully vent their feelings or voice their concerns, and if they ask for your input, offer your opinions or information. Do not, however, try to solve the problem yourself, circumventing the other person, and never offer to mediate a conflict unless both parties involved ask you to do so.

If you ever wonder if you have become "sucked in" or have become too involved, you probably have. Taking on problems that don't belong to you doesn't help the other person and is sure to bring stress, aggravation, and various other maladies to your life.

When you do for a man what he can and should do for himself you do him a disservice.

BENJAMIN FRANKLIN

SET UP A
HOME DESK
OR OFFICE
AREA

GIVE YOURSELF THE SPACE AND TOOLS TO MANAGE YOUR RESPONSIBILITIES SIMPLY AND EFFICIENTLY.

Organizing paperwork and information, managing a budget, and making short- and long-range plans are not tasks limited to business or work environments. These functions find their way into our homes as well.

Designate a place in your home that can function as an office. Ideally, the space should be practical, accessible, and pleasant. Recycle or purchase a desk or table to be used as a work surface, and invest in supplies, a good chair, and filing space. Be as functional or high-tech as you desire, and keep all your bills, receipts, etc. strictly confined to that area. Resist the temptation to use the kitchen table.

The clever do all things intelligently.

PROVERBS 13:16 NRSV

Throw Away the Leftovers I Know I will never Eat

DON'T STORE GUILT IN YOUR REFRIGERATOR.

Many of us were taught never to throw out food so we cling obsessively to those leftovers, oftentimes scooting them around in the refrigerator, lying to ourselves, until we feel we can justify throwing them away. What a head trip. If you or your family doesn't enjoy a dish, throw it out at the meal's end, and throw away the recipe with it.

For those leftovers you do enjoy, freeze uncooked portions to enjoy another day so you don't tire of the dish. Put a date on anything that is frozen or refrigerated, and use leftovers in a timely manner. It's amazing how complicated your life can become when you and your family all go down with a touch of food poisoning.

A warmed-up dinner was never worth much.

BOILEAU

CLOSE THE CURTAINS ON DISASTER

TO POSTPONE A PROBLEM TEMPORARILY CAN BE HELPFUL. TO DENY ITS EXISTENCE CAN LEAD TO DISASTER.

Each of us have times in our lives when we simply can't face the enormity of a problem. When that happens, we may need a little time, or a little distance from the situation. We need to give ourselves permission to close the curtain.

We should never live in denial. However, there are times when problems should be shelved for examination at a later time, and some things need to cool off before they are handled. Give yourself time to heal, adjust, and come up with a reasonable and workable plan. Forcing issues often leads to poor choices and complicated consequences.

If things go wrong, don't go with them.

ROGER BABSON

HOST POTLUCKS RATHER THAN DINNER PARTIES

124

SIMPLIFY YOUR ENTERTAINING— PUT THE EMPHASIS ON PEOPLE.

It isn't necessary to plan and cook a fancy dinner in order to entertain friends. Host a potluck dinner instead. Be prepared to provide the main dish and beverages, and then ask two or three friends or couples to bring side dishes—something they enjoy that complements the main dish. Encourage them to skip the work and purchase their dish at a deli or take-out restaurant of their choice!

Potlucks are usually long on taste and enjoyment, and short on preparation and cleanup. And, everyone takes his or her own pot home to wash.

They make their pride in making their dinner cost much; I make my pride in making my dinner cost little.

H.D. THOREAU

IF I REALLY WANTED TO SIMPLIFY MY LIFE, I WOULD . . .

KEEP TRACK OF MY CREDIT CARD SPENDING

CREDIT CARDS DON'T CREATE DEBT, BUT THEY DO FACILITATE IT.

In order to avoid the complications and confusion caused by credit card spending, use the same approach you use for check writing. Decide in advance what your budget can handle and post that amount in a separate check register. Each time you make a purchase, list the charge as if it were a check and subtract it from the budgeted amount. Remember to clip the receipt into the back of the register.

Credit card spending must be treated just like any other spending. Though the cash deduction is deferred, you are nevertheless creating an indebtedness. Debt complicates. Wise spending simplifies.

Let no debt remain outstanding, except the continuing debt to love one another, for he who loves his fellowman has fulfilled the law.

ROMANS 13:8

IF I REALLY WANTED TO
SIMPLIFY MY LIFE, I WOULD . . .

USE THE GRILL IN THE SUMMER

SIMPLE, FAST, AND GOOD MAKE A SIMPLY FABULOUS TRIO.

Those who are experts in grilling cite these benefits: family fun, streamlined preparation, less cooking time, fewer utensils, bowls, and pans needed, quick and easy cleanup, cooler and more pleasant surroundings, and fewer calories since grilling tends to burn away fat without loss of flavor and thus, less need for sauces and gravies.

Grilling is just one example of a technique that can save you time and energy while enhancing the quality of your life. Keep your eyes open for others that can make life less complex for yourself and those you love.

Simplicity is the badge of distinction and genius.

ALFRED A. MONTAPERT

GO FOR
DEPTH OVER
BREADTH

TO SIMPLY LIVE WELL, DIG DEEP INTO WHAT TRULY MATTERS.

Gold, silver, precious stones, oil, natural gas, and virtually all precious metals and minerals come from mining the depths of the earth. These precious substances tend to be in isolated pockets or veins and thus, mining requires hard work, careful planning, and courage. The results, however, produce genuine wealth, opportunity, and world standards of value.

So it is also with friendships, health, good marriages, faith, self-worth, hope, competency, a good reputation, and love. All these and the other great treasures of life require cultivation, diligence, discipline, and intensity of effort, but the result is an unfettered life of simplicity and worth. Focus on the real treasures of life.

The best portion of a good man's life is his little, nameless, unremembered acts of kindness and of love.

WILLIAM WORDSWORTH

PARE DOWN MY DAILY ROUTINE

DO LESS AND ENJOY IT MORE.

Think about what happens on days when you oversleep. You settle for accomplishing the bare essentials that will get you out of the door in a respectable state. Why not just live that way? A simpler morning routine, a simpler before-bed routine, a simpler hairstyle, clothing that is easy to care for, fewer possessions requiring daily maintenance, fewer obligations that require daily attention, a smaller garden to tend.

Take a close look at all that you do in a day and then look again for those things that are truly important. You need not lower your standards in terms of quality, only in terms of quantity.

Less is more.

ROBERT BROWNING

IF I REALLY WANTED TO
SIMPLIFY MY LIFE, I WOULD . . .

TURN OFF AS MUCH NOISE AS POSSIBLE

NOISE COMPLICATES; SILENCE SIMPLIFIES.

I f you are having trouble hearing yourself think, you might try turning off the television set, the compact disk player, the video recorder, the radio, the tape deck, the computer, the printer, the phone, the beeper, and the pager. Close the door or window on the traffic and the neighborhood leaf blowers. Push the stop buttons on all whirring, chopping, grinding, or swishing appliances, and ask others in your home to use headphones or engage in silent activities to help create a totally quiet zone.

The silence may be deafening at first, but you'll come to love it once you realize that silence nourishes introspection, stimulates creativity, and fosters mental and emotional well-being.

In quietness and trust is your strength.

ISAIAH 30:15

IF I REALLY WANTED TO SIMPLIFY MY LIFE, I WOULD . . .

THINK THROUGH DECISIONS CAREFULLY

TAKE YOUR TIME AND MAKE GOOD CHOICES, OR WASTE YOUR TIME RECOVERING FROM BAD ONES.

Any car salesman will tell you that it's much easier to sell something to someone who doesn't know what he wants or how much he can afford to pay. It's just human nature to let the excitement of the moment short circuit the decision making process.

It's simply wise to do your homework and weigh your options before making any major decision, such as changing jobs, marrying, moving to a new state, or making a large purchase. You can seriously complicate your life by choosing a particular path before you are absolutely certain what you want and what you don't want. Take time to be sure.

Sometimes your best investments are the ones you don't make.

DONALD TRUMP

STAY FOCUSED ON THE TRULY IMPORTANT THINGS IN MY LIFE

A LITTLE PERSPECTIVE GOES A LONG WAY.

Take a few minutes to reflect on what you consider to be the top five priorities of your life. Write them down and keep the list in your wallet. When little hassles threaten to derail your day, take a moment to pull out your list.

As you consider each item, ask yourself how the struggle or crisis you are currently experiencing will impact the priorities on your list. If you determine that they will not be affected, abandon, table, or resolve the situation immediately. Don't spend additional time on something you are likely to consider a waste of time five years from now. Don't complicate your life fretting over temporary problems.

If people concentrated on the really important things in life, there'd be a shortage of fishing poles.

DOUG LARSON

KEEP SEPARATE HAMPERS FOR WHITE AND COLORED LAUNDRY

WHERE THERE'S A WILL, THERE'S A WAY.

Color is one of the first distinctions we learn to make in life. Most every member of the family should be able to successfully separate their darks from their lights. So why leave that for someone else to do?

Make everyone in your family responsible for putting their soiled white and colored garments into separate hampers or laundry baskets. Keep a third sack, hamper, or basket for items that must be dry cleaned. Mark the hampers and remember to keep them in the same place. Of course, you will have to double check, but in a short time you should find that laundry day is easier for everyone.

Every problem contains the seeds of its own solution.

NORMAN VINCENT PEALE

CHOOSE FIDELITY

THE FAITHFUL NEVER NEED TO FEAR EXPOSURE.

F idelity means the faithful execution of your duty, obligations, or vows. It means that when faced with a choice, you choose not to lie, cheat, steal, commit adultery, or harm another person. It means that when you say you will do something, you do it. Living a life of fidelity means that you do not have to cover your behavior with alibis, take evasive action to avoid certain people, or devise elaborate schemes to make amends.

Unfaithfulness is complicated. It requires an unusually large expenditure of energy and effort. It can lead to broken relationships, physical and emotional pain, and loss of reputation. In the end, it pays to do the right thing.

The Lord preserves the faithful.

PSALM 31:23 NKJV

IF I REALLY WANTED TO
SIMPLIFY MY LIFE, I WOULD . . .

BE FLEXIBLE
ABOUT WHAT IS
NOT IMPORTANT

IF YOU DON'T DECIDE WHO YOU
ARE, SOMEONE ELSE WILL DECIDE
FOR YOU.

Determine what issues in your life are non-negotiable and allow the rest to be subject to negotiation and compromise. That way you will have a personal guideline for when to stand firm and when you might be flexible and defer to the tastes and desires of others. Make these decisions in a quiet time of reflection, not when you are under pressure or in a crisis.

It is important that your choices reflect your thinking and are not influenced by the thinking of others. If you are trying to please others, you will not be able to fully commit to your choices as priorities. Decisions are simpler for those who are true to themselves.

Choose your battles. You win the war by
winning the important ones.

ANONYMOUS

MAKE LUNCHES THE NIGHT BEFORE

GETTING "READY" AND "SET" THE NIGHT BEFORE MAKES "GO" AN EASIER TASK IN THE MORNING.

Why leave one more task for the early morning routine? This is one chore you can easily take care of ahead of time. Prepare as many lunch items as possible the night before—mix up sandwich fillings, put salads in individual serving containers, put cut-up veggies and finger foods in plastic baggies, and put any utensils, napkins, and condiments into the lunch bags.

Since the morning schedule offers a limited number of minutes with little room for error, it's easy to squeeze this task out when there isn't time to do everything. That can mean you must eat lunch out or not at all.

Dig the well before you are thirsty.

CHINESE PROVERB

REFUSE TO START WHAT I CANNOT FINISH

HAVE THE FINISH LINE IN FULL VIEW BEFORE YOU GO TO THE STARTING LINE.

T aking on more than they can handle is a way of life for many people. Sure they have good intentions, but good intentions count for very little when the job is only half done. Commitment, perseverance, and long-suffering are the traits required to see a job through to completion. Being a finisher may not sound as exciting as being a mover and a shaker who starts multiple new ventures, but finishers have the satisfaction of knowing that they got the job done.

Unfinished projects will complicate your life and serve as distractions and detours. Finished projects build competency and confidence in your life and serve as stepping stones to greater success.

You begin well in nothing except you end well.

THOMAS FULLER, M. D.

INSTALL A FAMILY MESSAGE BOARD

BEING LOVED IS A BIG RESPONSIBILITY.

One of the best ways to establish good communication in your home and eliminate wasted time and motion through mixed signals or failed-to-deliver messages is to establish a family message board. Each person should be urged to use it to tell other family members where they are, when they will be back, who has phoned, etc. Family message boards can also be used to send more general messages such as "I love you," or "I'm praying for you."

Keeping in touch with one another is basically a common courtesy that acknowledges the care and concern we feel for the safety and well-being of those we live with. It also promotes a sense of belonging and discourages misunderstandings.

Communication is central to a family's success.
Without communication there is no family.

ANONYMOUS

IF I REALLY WANTED TO
SIMPLIFY MY LIFE, I WOULD . . .

COMBINE
MY ERRAND
RUNS

WHY PUT OFF UNTIL TOMORROW WHAT YOU CAN DO TODAY?

I n our age of convenience stores and quick transportation, we tend to think that errands are of little consequence when it comes to time. But unorganized errand runs can still take longer than organized ones, and shopping for one item at a time, especially at a convenience store, can be costly.

Group your errands together, making the most of your mileage and time. This approach encourages the use of coupons and buying in bulk, which can make a big difference in your grocery bill. But the greatest advantage is that an errand day can make a number of other days errand free.

I recommend you take care of the minutes, for the hours will take care of themselves.

LORD CHESTERFIELD

LEAVE WHERE-YOU-CAN-FIND-ME INFORMATION WITH MULTIPLE PEOPLE

INFORMATION IS POWER—USE IT TO BUY PEACE OF MIND.

One of the most annoying and anxiety-ridden aspects of a crisis is generally this: not being able to find a key person. It just makes sense to leave information about your whereabouts with several people. "Here's where I'll be" and "here's how to reach me" information provides security for those you are leaving behind and peace of mind for you, in that you know you can be reached in the event of an emergency.

Be wise and keep the lines of communication wide open. It is possible to be no more than a telephone call away from those you love—if they can find the number.

Knowledge is of two kinds: we know a subject ourselves or we know where we can find information upon it.

SAMUEL JOHNSON

Choose Good-Quality, Low-Maintenance Products and Reputable Service Providers

IT'S SIMPLY SMARTER TO INSIST ON QUALITY AND RELIABILITY.

Save yourself time, money, and frustration by choosing the very best quality you can afford in both goods and services. The benefits are many: less time and money spent taking items to and from repair shops and less time lost while items are being repaired or serviced; less effort repairing faulty items, remedying faulty service, or attempting to work around flaws.

A man once calculated that over a five-year period he spent more than $200 in repairs on a vacuum cleaner that he had purchased on discount. A new model at full price cost less than $200! Finding items at a bargain or on sale can be a real blessing, but never if quality has been sacrificed.

A man loseth his time who comes early to a had bargain.

THOMAS FULLER

Install a Board for Keys

WHERE ARE YOUR KEYS? RIGHT WHERE YOU LEFT THEM!

Many people have speculated at one time or another that there is a Land of Lost Socks that exists out there, somewhere. Some have speculated further that it is located near the Halfway House for Lost Keys. Much time and anxiety can be saved by putting keys in a place where you can find them quickly.

Don't provide yet another opportunity for jangled nerves and utter frustration. Life is too short. And make sure your key board holds an extra key for every car in the family. When you dash out to an appointment and find that someone has parked behind you and then disappeared, you'll be glad you did.

Common sense is not so common.

VOLTAIRE

IF I REALLY WANTED TO
SIMPLIFY MY LIFE, I WOULD . . .

TRUST GOD

WHY WORRY WHEN YOU CAN PRAY?

L ife can be a frightening, difficult, lonely, and complex experience. Isn't it good to know that there is someone who watches over us and never leaves us in the best and the worst of it all? You can simplify your life today by placing your cares in the hollow of God's hand.

The Bible quotes the Psalmist who said, "I will lift my eyes unto the hills from whence cometh my help. My help cometh from the Lord, which made heaven and earth (Psalm 121:1-2 KJV)." These words were penned by a man who knew the peace and comfort of resting in the care of Someone greater than himself. That same peace and comfort is available to all those who ask for it.

Blessed are all they that put their trust in Him.

PSALM 2:12 KJV

www.ingramcontent.com/pod-product-compliance
Lightning Source LLC
Chambersburg PA
CBHW070712130626
46553CB00005B/1950